WORKING TOWARDS EQUALITY

What Is AGEISM?

Sarah Harvey

Explore other books at:
WWW.ENGAGEBOOKS.COM

VANCOUVER, B.C

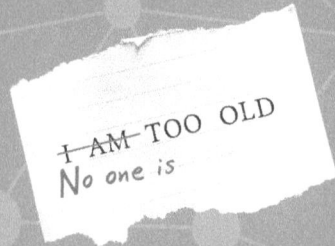 WWW.ENGAGEBOOKS.COM

What Is Ageism? - Working Towards Equality: Level 3
Harvey, Sarah 1950 –
Text © 2023 Engage Books
Design © 2023 Engage Books

Edited by: A.R. Roumanis, Ashley Lee, and Melody Sun
Design by: Mandy Christiansen

Text set in Montserrat Regular.
Chapter headings set in Merlo Neue.

FIRST EDITION / FIRST PRINTING

Every reasonable effort has been made to contact the copyright holders of all material reproduced in this book. Image on page 13 from Clairebendavid. Image on page 25 from Fraktion DIE LINKE. im Bundestag.

LIBRARY AND ARCHIVES CANADA CATALOGUING IN PUBLICATION

Title: What is ageism? / Sarah Harvey.
Names: Harvey, Sarah N., 1950- author.
Description: Series statement: Working towards equality

Identifiers: Canadiana (print) 20230447562 | Canadiana (ebook) 20230447570
ISBN 978-1-77476-867-9 (hardcover)
ISBN 978-1-77476-868-6 (softcover)
ISBN 978-1-77476-869-3 (epub)
ISBN 978-1-77476-870-9 (pdf)
ISBN 978-1-77878-128-5 (audio)

Subjects:
LCSH: Ageism—Juvenile literature.

Classification: LCC HQ1061 .H38 2023 | DDC J305.2—DC23

This project has been made possible in part by the Government of Canada.

Canada

Contents

What Is Ageism?

Ageism means treating people poorly because of their age. Ageism mostly affects older people. Older women are more likely to experience ageism than older men.

Aging is **universal** and natural. But many people believe that getting older is something people should feel bad about. About one in two people around the world are ageist towards older people.

Universal:
affecting everybody.

AGE LIMIT 35

Ageism and Health

People who see aging as a bad thing are less likely to take care of themselves as they get older. They may stop going out or seeing other people. This can lead to physical and mental health problems.

People who are ageist live 7.5 years less than those who are not.

Older people often do not get the healthcare they need because of ageism. Some people do not think older people's problems are as important as younger people's problems. They may be talked down to or not given any attention.

The History of Ageism 1

Ageism has a long history. Youth was prized in Ancient Greece and Rome, but old age was not. A Roman named Seneca once wrote, "Old age is an incurable disease." Incurable means something is not able to be fixed.

In the early 1900s, **factories** became popular, and people stopped making things by hand. Factory owners thought older people would not be able to learn how to work in factories. They would only hire young people. They would force people to stop working once they reached a certain age.

Factories: places where machines are used to make things people can buy.

The History of Ageism 2

In 1967, the United States passed the Age Discrimination in Employment Act. This made it against the law for businesses to **discriminate** against older people who work for them. The law protects people over the age of 40.

KEY WORD

Discriminate: treat someone badly because they are part of a certain group of people.

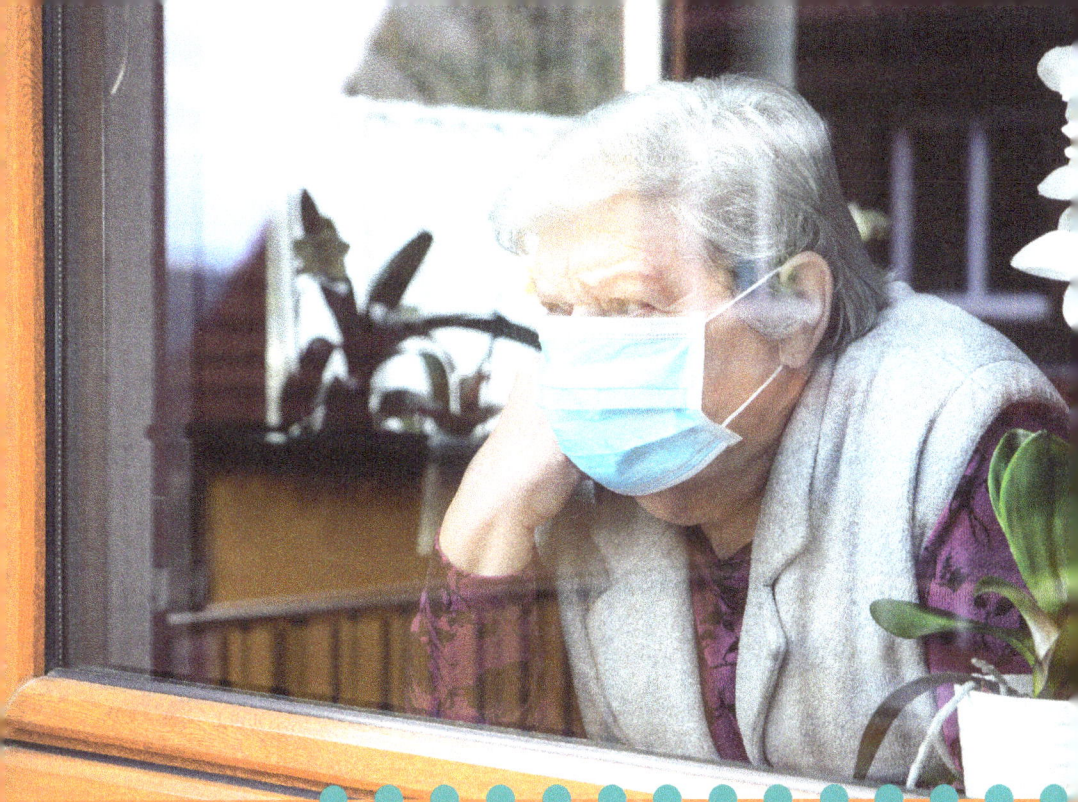

Older people were often treated poorly during the COVID-19 **pandemic** in 2020 to 2023. Many people thought the stay-at-home orders were in place because of older people. They thought older people were making life harder for everyone else.

KEY WORD

Pandemic: when a bad illness spreads to many countries around the world.

Why Are Some People Ageist?

Children learn to be ageist by living in a **culture** where ageism is accepted. They hear their parents or other kids being ageist and think it is okay. They may also see ageism in movies, books, or TV, or on social media.

KEY WORD

Culture: the values, beliefs, and behaviors of a group of people.

12

People are living longer now than they ever have before. This is because of better medicine. As the number of older people grows, so does ageism.

What Does Ageism Look Like?

Some people believe that older people are weak or cannot learn new things. These are harmful **stereotypes**. People may make jokes about stereotypes or treat people differently because of them.

KEY WORD

Stereotypes: unfair or untrue beliefs about a person or a group of people.

Ageist comments can often sound well-meaning. People do not know they are being ageist. They may say someone looks good for their age. But this is based on the idea that older people must look a certain way.

Everybody ages differently. No two people age in the exact same way.

Aging and Cultures

People from different cultures think about aging in different ways. **Indigenous** people treat older people with care and respect. Older people share their life experiences and knowledge with young people.

Indigenous: the first people to live in a place.

Older people are also respected in many Asian cultures. In Korea, people celebrate when they turn 60 or 70 years old. They have big parties with their families.

What to Do if You See or Experience Ageism 1

You may hear someone making ageist comments to an older person. Ask yourself if the older person really does need or want help. It is ageist to think they cannot handle the situation on their own because of their age.

Try to stay calm when speaking to someone about ageism.

If someone does need help and you feel comfortable, ask the person making comments if they know they are being ageist. They may not know. This could be a good time to teach them about ageism.

What to Do if You See or Experience Ageism 2

If you do not feel comfortable talking to the person who is being ageist, try to get the older person away from them. Take them somewhere quiet. Stay by their side so they know they are not alone.

If you feel unsafe, find another adult who can help.

Hearing ageist comments can make a person sad or angry. Support the older person as best you can. Ask them if there is anything you can do to help them feel better.

Superheroes Against Ageism in the Past

Robert Butler was a doctor who studied aging. He came up with the term "ageism" in 1969. He spent many years making sure people knew about ageism. He also fought for the fair treatment of older people.

Barbara Robb started a group called Aid to the Elderly in Government Institutions (AEGIS) in 1965. The group fought for older people to be treated better in hospitals. Barbara gave ideas on how to make care for older people better in her book, *Sans Everything*.

Superheroes Against Ageism Today

Michelle Yeoh is an actress who is fighting against the belief that older women can no longer act. She won an Oscar for her acting in the movie *Everything Everywhere All at Once*. She has spoken out about how older women can do many of the things younger women can.

Margaret Morganroth Gullette has been fighting against ageism for years. She wrote a book in 2017 called *Ending Ageism, or How Not to Shoot Old People*. In her book, she explains how ageism affects all of **society** and says people need to stop letting it happen.

Claudia Mahler is an Independent Expert on the enjoyment of all human rights by older persons. This means she helps governments stop ageism. She was given this title by the United Nations Human Rights Council in May 2020.

Ways to Support Change 1

Avoid using the word "elderly" and saying that older people are weak. Try not to use the word "still" when discussing older people. They are not still working. They are just working.

"Aging is not 'lost youth' but a new stage of opportunity and strength."
—Betty Frieden

Ask a teacher or librarian to help you find books that celebrate all ages. Try to learn from them. Share what you learn with friends and family.

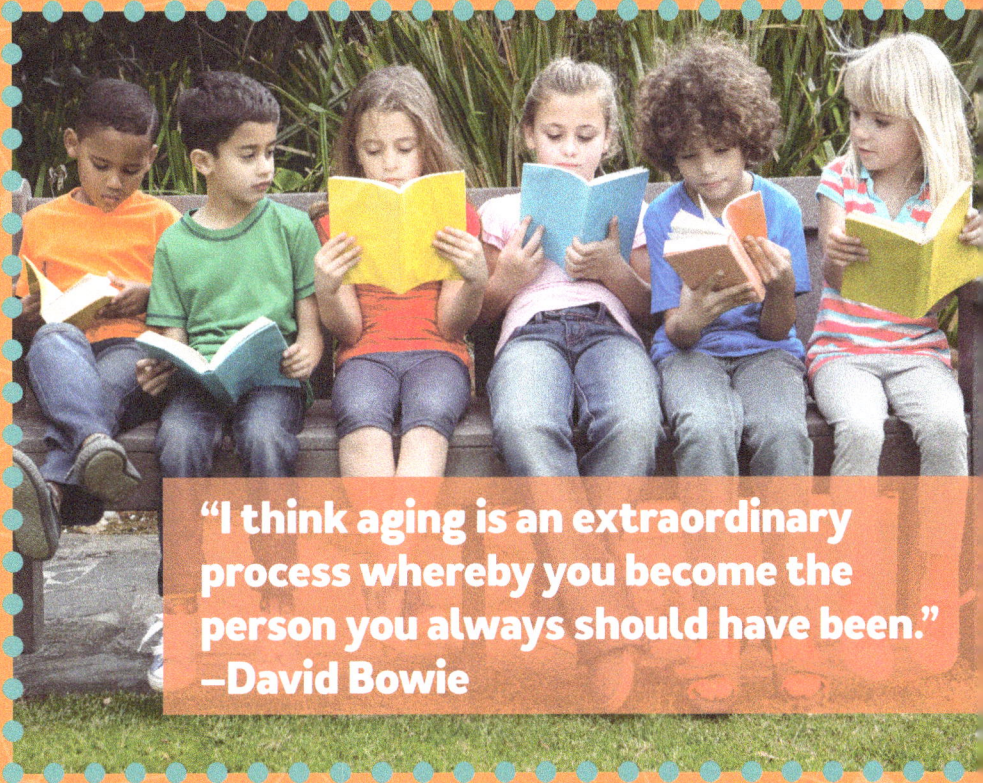

"I think aging is an extraordinary process whereby you become the person you always should have been." –David Bowie

Ways to Support Change 2

Call out ageism when you see it on social media or in movies or TV. Learning to spot ageism online or on TV will help you spot it in real life. It can also help you to better understand what ageism looks like.

"Age is just a number. Life and aging are the greatest gifts that we could possibly ever have." –Cicely Tyson

Spend time with your grandparents or other older people. Find things you have in common. Kids who spend time with older people are less likely to be ageist when they get older.

Quiz

Test your knowledge of ageism by answering the following questions. The questions are based on what you have read in this book. The answers are listed on the bottom of the next page.

1 What is ageism?

2 Is aging natural?

3 What does the word "discriminate" mean?

4 How do children learn to be ageist?

5 What are stereotypes?

6 What is the name of the group Barbara Robb started?

Explore Other Level 3 Readers.

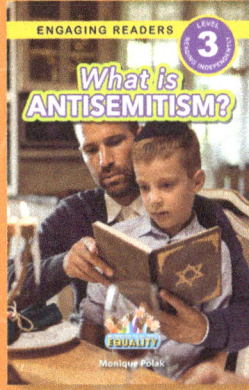

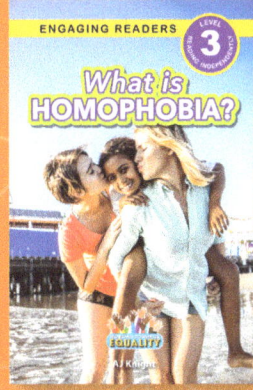

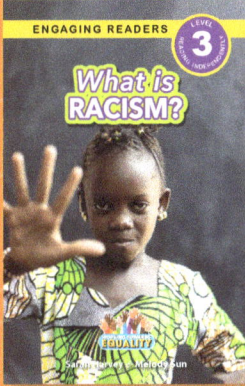

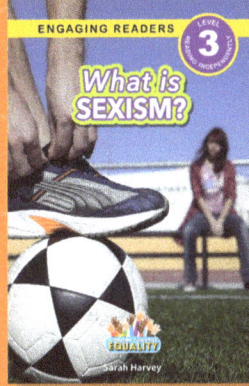

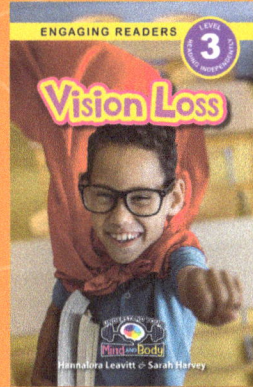

ENGAGING READERS — LEVEL 3
What is ABLEISM?
EQUALITY
Adelaide Wilde

ENGAGING READERS — LEVEL 3
What is ANTISEMITISM?
EQUALITY
Monique Polak

ENGAGING READERS — LEVEL 3
What is HOMOPHOBIA?
EQUALITY
AJ Knight

ENGAGING READERS — LEVEL 3
What is RACISM?
EQUALITY
Melody Sun

ENGAGING READERS — LEVEL 3
What is SEXISM?
EQUALITY
Sarah Harvey

ENGAGING READERS — LEVEL 3
Diabetes
Mind and Body
Kit Caudron-Robinson

ENGAGING READERS — LEVEL 3
Obesity
Mind and Body
Kit Caudron-Robinson

ENGAGING READERS — LEVEL 3
Autism
Mind and Body
AJ Knight

ENGAGING READERS — LEVEL 3
Vision Loss
Mind and Body
Hannalora Leavitt & Sarah Harvey

Visit www.engagebooks.com/readers

Answers: 1. Treating people poorly because of their age 2. Yes 3. To treat someone badly because they are part of a certain group of people 4. By living in a culture where ageism is accepted 5. Unfair or untrue beliefs about a person or a group of people 6. Aid to the Elderly in Government Institutions